Guidance From Beyond

A book of channelled writing from many different sources

Tina Hunt

authorHOUSE®

AuthorHouse™ UK Ltd.
500 Avebury Boulevard
Central Milton Keynes, MK9 2BE
www.authorhouse.co.uk
Phone: 08001974150

First published by AuthorHouse   5/6/2011

ISBN: 978-1-4567-7549-0 (sc)
ISBN: 978-1-4567-7550-6 (e)

Artwork by Josephine Jones

Contents

INTENTION

What is it that you desire?
Search your Soul, and ask ~ What do you need that can best serve **you**?
Be Concise ~ be clear.
Make it known to the Universe, *What* you desire, and stay focused.
Be positive ~ be optimistic.
Do not allow doubt to come in.
Think about your desires.
Speak the words *out loud*.
Act upon the decisions.
Keep your mind in the present, and know that you shall receive.
Give *Thanks* to the Universe ~ Always!

COURAGE

We watch with interest, as Humans are beginning to stop and take a closer look at themselves, to question and to seek answers. For so long, they have walked blindly, refusing to take responsibility for their actions. It is a wondrous sight when we see a tiny, flicker of Light, become a flame that shines brightly. How we rejoice, and yet we fully understand, how difficult it is to separate one's self from the crowd. It takes Courage to be an individual, and begin to search within. We often do not like what we see, and it is a challenge to face our fears. When you open your hearts and minds, and allow The Light to flood in, it will bring you all the strength and courage you need, to face all your fears. The Light is pure Love, and you can re-connect with your Divine Self within The Light. Take Courage with both hands, and let the Divineness within, flow through every part of your Being. Let your Spirit shine, and your Souls will grow and blossom: become at one with all that is.

ILLUSIONS AND ILLUMINATIONS

It is better to seek within, for all earthly life is an illusion.
The Light which is Truth and Knowledge is within.
All you ever need to know is within.
Illuminate the Soul, shine your Light, and you will receive
all the answers. Each Soul walks it's own path, and it is not
for another to guide you. Only you and your Higher Self,
that greater part of you that does not incarnate, knows what
is best and can guide you, to take the right pathway in life.
Seek the Divine within, and you will shine.
You will be illuminated for all to see.

NOURISHMENT FOR THE SOUL

All things that are living need to be replenished. Our physical bodies need to be nourished with food and water. If we fail to give regular attention to ourselves, then we fall into ill-health. It is a natural progression.

And so it is with the Soul, our living counterpart ~ the Spirit within. We must nourish it with Love and Kindness. Give it every attention. It too suffers with neglect. Feed it with thoughts of Light and Positivity, and random acts of Goodness. Follow your heart's guidance and listen to the inner voice - your Conscience. Be guided by your feelings and your intuition, what some have termed *a gut feeling*. When something feels good and right, then you are going with your intuition. That *inner knowing* is your Higher Self, that part of your Soul that remains in Spirit. It is the purpose of each Sojourn upon the Earth, to overcome the lower Self, and rise up to be with our Higher Selves. There must be balance and harmony. We must give equal attention to the Mind, Body *and* Soul. If we create imbalance and dis-harmony, then dis-ease will surely follow.

Bless You.

PREPARATION FOR THE COMING OF THE LIGHT

It filters through the many channels that are opening up. It has been a continuous trickle, but now is the *time* for *The Light* to flood the Earth.
Be prepared.
Awaken now, and listen to the urgings of your Soul.
Do not heed what others say to you.
Go within, be still, be quiet.
Listen to the *inner voice* the quiet one: listen to your heart.
Stop! Review your Life situation, and *change* what you know to be wrong!
Put things right ***now!***

It is time to take responsibility!

CONTEMPLATION

Why should you still the mind, with it's never-ending and ceaseless chatter?

Without the silence, it is not possible to still the mind. It goes round and round.

Be still, be quiet, focus on the breath.

Action, not in-action.

This is the course you must take. Stop dilly dallying around.

   Make a decision and stick by it. It is not difficult. Focus.

LIFE IN SPIRIT - *from a Mother*

The vistas are supreme beyond comprehension. You could never imagine the glory or the beauty. Greetings from many of us here in the World of Spirit. We come with love and laughter. So often the silence surrounding you should be broken with laughter.

As I passed from this life, it was like a light sleep, almost a dream. I felt myself drifting, but I had no desire to stay. I knew what was happening and I was happy. The relief from pain was a blessing. I woke in a room filled with Light. At first I thought I was dreaming, but then I recognised my loved-ones who were all standing around. They had all come to greet me.

What a to-do! Everyone seemed to be talking at once. And yet they were just smiling. It was serene, yet alarming, as the realisation hit me. My thoughts drifted back to you and my son. I felt saddened to be gone from your lives, but a sense of relief washed over me as I drifted into a deep and peaceful sleep.

Each time I woke, someone was there watching over me, attending to my needs, which seemed only to be of comforting me. All to soon the moment arrived when I knew it was time to move on. I found myself by a pool of water. We walked down steps into the warm healing, water, my garments floating around me. I felt warm, secure in the knowledge I could rest a while. I was tired, but the surroundings were blissful. So much love to give and receive.

I had lost track of time. I didn't know if days or weeks or even hours, had passed ~ it seemed unimportant. My companion at my side spoke of a need to return to the

Earth Planes for a while if I desired it. We watched you with heavy hearts ~ so many tears.

I want to thank you from the bottom of my heart, for the loving send-off. I appreciated the flowers, and I was overwhelmed with the love. I felt it. Many thanks to you all, I will carry that memory with me. I did it *My way*, as you know.

What joy to be free at last. How long I waited, a part of me wanting to stay, but how I longed to leave my wretched body. I felt like a prisoner.

Day after day I prayed, but it was not to be so. I resigned myself to completing *my shift* with a stiff upper lip, a call of duty. Nowadays, life is full of pleasure, no bodily functions to attend to, free to move at will, engaging in past-times I never dreamed of.

Regrets, I had a few... (sung!)

So much time wasted, precious time.

I urge you to fulfil your dreams and desires. Don't wait , until it's too late, as I did. What you cannot complete can be continued on this side of life at your leisure, no hurry. Days are filled with pleasure or activities, and of course there is always work to be done, if you wish.

I like to be with the little children. Sometimes they are sad, or distressed, but in time they come to understand, and then they in turn help others.

It is healing of the mind that is paramount here, for the physical has been left behind. Although we have bodies *so to speak*, we just float about - they have no needs. We can eat and drink if we so wish, but after a time we understand that this is not necessary. We spend our time with others whom we love.

My husband and I are inseparable. Sometimes when he is

away working on other planes of life, I am still comforted by his presence. My sisters often visit with us, and we reminisce about old days. Only it is so much simpler here. It is not emotional. There is a knowing, an understanding of life, of what has been. No need for words, as you and I would have done.

Think not of us as having gone. We are closer than you think. Just a thought away. Love is the essence that binds us all together. We are not separate. We are as one, for ever and always.

Treat each other with kindness. Wrong action will bring regret. Watch out for others. We are all in this together ~ remember this.

TIL WE MEET AGAIN....

How I hung on! The fear of letting go. The pain on one hand, but I feared the abyss ~ how foolish of me. I wanted to believe what you had told me. In the end he came for me. He held out his hand. Reassured, I took it, and followed him. What an incredible journey! As if sleep-walking we travelled through mists of time, into the Light. My dream come true ~ together again.

So many times I had whispered those words, *'til we meet again.* A part of me knowing, but always my mind dragging me away from the Truth. What a comfort you were. Steady as a rock. I will cherish that, always. You girls will never know, just to hear your voices in that empty space ~ trapped in a pain-wracked body, your voices floating in the air, knowing you were there.

Time passes by so quickly here, it is difficult to keep track as there is no desire to do so. We congregate in huge halls, many, many people, all with one purpose ~ to love, and be loved. You could not comprehend the feeling here. There are no words to describe such fulfilment. The music is exquisite. The sights and sounds are indescribable. Melody floats in the air, tinkling sweetly in my ear, flowers singing to me as I tend our garden. Our home is everything I dreamed of. We are together again. Patiently he waited until my time to return home. So happy you will be ~ no cigarettes for me, just tea! (laughing!)

What to say to you ~ as you know I visit with you often, trying to impress my thoughts upon you, playing with your hair. You know that I am there.

But where is the stillness that you need, where you would hear me ~ that small voice within. Don't dismiss the words

you hear. Listen carefully, I will guide your footsteps.
Everyone here sending thoughts of love, no need for letter
writing here. It is as if the word spoken in the mind, is
received before it is heard. Just *think* yourself somewhere,
and it will be...... so easy now but I struggled in the
beginning. Others helped me. Learning to trust is the key.
Now I can be wherever I wish. So often at your side.
My children, you are not forgotten. I can do more for you
now. Forgive me, as I forgive myself.
Allow yourselves to let go. Know that *we will meet again!*
Make the most of the time allotted to you on the Earth
plane; so many opportunities. Don't be blinded by false
thinking. Listen to your hearts. Be guided from within.
You will fare well. Only time will tell if I speak the truth.
I come to you from a place of Love, understand this and
you will remember. We are not so far away. Just a thought,
a vibration. It's so easy to hear us, if you only took the
time. So much to do, so little time given to what really
matters in life. There is no death. We are more *alive* than
you. We surround you, as you surround us; as above, so
below. Without and within, there is no difference. It just is
~ life is everlasting. It continues. Life goes on.
Your Grandmother is here with me now. She has been
speaking to you. I know you were aware of the change in
energies. She comes with so much love for you. She knows
your heart. She follows your daily life with keen interest.
Keep on the pathway you have chosen for yourself. Your
feet are firmly planted, so to speak.
You have developed am ability to communicate, like many
others around you. This is the way forward.
We appreciate greatly, the difficulties you experience, but
you will succeed. Have no doubt about that. There is no

hurry, all is going to plan.

Out of this turmoil and chaos will come order, it is natural law. There can be no other outcome. What will be will be. I reach out to you daughter, with outstretched arms. Tears flowing for unspoken words and wrong action. If only I had listened to my heart, but with the mind closed, God can only wait patiently for His Children to awaken once again. So much time wasted, but I am making up for it now. I accept the help I am given, from loved-ones around me. There has been no separation, just an empty space, which you will cross when the time comes. Meanwhile I will walk with you, guiding your footsteps as my Mother did before me. Know that we are here with you, helping you, you are never alone, When you send out just one thought to us we are by your side in an instant. To watch over you and support you. There can be no greater gift than a Mothers love. How I regret the mistakes I made. But I have learned, as you will learn from yours, my child. Your ability to express the love you feel has been a saving grace. This I am learning to do. Tell them *we will meet again.* Love binds us together. We are all connected. One big family. I can care more for you now, on this side of life than I was able to do when I was on the Earth. Peace be with you.

Love always, Mum.

A FATHER SPEAKS

Where to begin? Life here is blissful! Opportunities for one's progress, or one can just rest for a while, and take it all in. Thank you for the chance to speak with you, I have been waiting patiently in the wings, watching you progress ~ sometimes with difficulties So many interruptions along your pathway, but at least it is clearing.

Please take the time to sit quietly in the garden to commune with us. Only time will show you what you can achieve, what you may accomplish. We assist you in any way that we can, but you must meet us halfway.

Life here is multi-layered. By that I mean that you can be all things ~ whatever you desire. You must create harmony and balance here, then what your heart desires, can become reality. At first it is a struggle, after being on the Earth planes, but if you wish to progress to higher planes of vibration, then you must apply yourself. It is not difficult, once you become accustomed to the many levels of being. Myself, I am able to move from one plane of existence, to another, with ease.

Bless You

Dad

LITTLE GEMS

Do unto others as you would have others do unto you.
Spiritual laws must be followed. They are what matters.
Your man-made laws have no power here. Love all,
God Bless, Goodnight.

Love, Light and Blessings.
Come, step forward and be counted.
Now is the time to prepare for what must be achieved.

Each time we draw close to you, we strengthen the bond,
which is a Bond of Love. We are privileged to work with
you, and it pleases us greatly, to be given the opportunity.

Greater powers than Man exist on the Earth. The two must
come together as one. Man has resisted for too long, and it
is imperative that the Soul of Man moves on.

Mother Earth is our keeper. She holds us close to her heart.
She enfolds us in her bosom. Let us be a part of her very
Soul. Why do we struggle and separate ourselves? Life is
one pulse, one heart beating. We must re-align ourselves,
make an adjustment, and be as One once more.

The colours of The Rainbow are infused with pure energy.
Replicate these colours whenever and wherever you can.

Welcome to the world of creativity. Once you get started,
the energy will begin to flow and you will take off. Mark
my words!

WORDS OF ENCOURAGEMENT

Life is like a continuous circle, moving forward you can step on or off at your leisure, so that you maintain the pace that is right for you. What works for one person, may not be right for another. Perseverance is the key. Keep on trying, until you get it right.

You must be comfortable with what you are doing.
Do not try to wear another person's shoes ~ stick to your own style. Do not be afraid to ask questions~ even of yourself.
Be true to yourself, know in your heart what you wish, then work towards a goal.
Never be afraid to try something new and exciting.
Challenge yourself.
Step out of your comfort zone.
Have self-respect, honour yourself.
You are important, you are what matters.
Do not be afraid to do things for *you*, put yourself first.
Ask, *what will this do for me?*
Treat others how you would expect them to treat you.
Face up to your failures, use them as a guide, a measuring stick.
Learn from any mistakes and move on.
Do not dwell on what might have been.
Keep looking forward.
With right action, you will fulfil your destiny.
Good Luck!

WORK TO BE DONE FOR ONE'SELF.

Meditate Daily, this is all we ask of you.
Drink water , it is most important.
Eat well, and eat healthily. Eat what is good for you,
always.
Life is about choices. Think again, if you wish to change.
The Choice is yours!
Clear your mind.
Let Go.
Release all the old fears.
Recognise them for what they are.
Free yourself.
There are no barriers, only what you create.
Think again.
Clear your space, create balance.
Have patience.
Nurture and be kind to yourself.
Never mind the desires of others.
  Consider their views and opinions, and follow your Truth
always.

THE SOUL

Let us begin with the Light within.
It guides you and never falters.
Pray for stillness, so that you may hear the quiet voice
within.
Too often drowned by the deafening sound of silence, or
the chattering of your minds.
The Soul knows what is best for you, let it feed your mind,
with Wisdom, and your heart with Love.
Override it's guidance at your peril.
You will suffer the consequences of foolish actions.
Listen to your Soul, it knows you, it *is* you.
Your Soul and you are One.
Love and honour yourself.

Bless You.

CHANGE

The state of unconscious beings on The Earth must *Change*.
Acceptance is paramount. The Human Spirit is evolving,
and Mankind must go with the flow. He cannot and must
not resist. Resistance is futile. Compatibility is the key,
and we are moving closer to this day by day. Give your
Souls permission to re-connect with The Source of All Life.
Do what makes you happy ~ always.
Lift yourselves up.
Think good thoughts.
Say kind words.
Do loving actions. Help others ~ heal yourself.

A MESSAGE TO A GROUP OF LIGHT CIRCLE WORKERS

The work has been done very well. You are a group of well-intentioned Souls. The Light has been anchored in that area now, and will continue to spread. Thank you for your efforts and the good work you have accomplished. It is needed that more Humans take up this work, if the Earth is to continue her ascension with ease. The Light is steadily increasing, and this is due to the efforts of many Souls on the Earth. Take control of yourselves. Centre yourselves. Bring in The Light and empower yourselves

TO BE LIGHT WORKERS

Those who choose to work must become more aware of their inner bodies. They must centre themselves, open their hearts and expand their consciousnesses, so they can bring in The Light. By doing this, they are raising their own energy, and increasing that of the Earth too. It is imperative, that relaxation is done first, to maximise the work and effort, of those sitting.

Bless You.

Now is the time we must heal the Earth, and we can start by healing ourselves. As our Light increases, so too, will the Light of the Earth. All is well, all will be well.

We must be positive in our thinking. It is no longer acceptable to bury our heads in the sand, and assume that someone else, or something will do it for us. Light Workers must shine their Lights, and show others the way. We must be still and go within, for inner guidance, become truly aware and be present in the *now*.

We are here with you as you seek to aid The Light. We are many in number and Love is all we need to succeed.

WISDOM

Wisdom is the reward one receives when seeking spiritual Truths. When one is confronted with contradicting information, it can be confusing and off-putting to the Seeker. But those who struggle on, sorting the wheat from the chaff, are *rewarded* for their determination, discipline and commitment. It is a difficult path to walk. Far easier to turn one's back and continue blindly through the maze of life.

Our concerns are many, so few of you take up the challenge and much time is wasted. Endless hours are spent in the pursuit of pleasure and entertainment. Such little time is given to the growth and progress of the Soul. The purpose of life. It is paramount that Humans bring balance into their lives, and begin to pay attention to the spiritual body as well, not just the physical. Too often, the emotional body rages out of control, and wreaks havoc. Go within, and listen to your heart. It guides you well.

The Eternal Divine Spark

A gentle light,

that burns so bright,

will guide you onwards,

day and night.

From the first day that you were born,

the flame has weathered every storm.

Your journey began

when you took your first breath,

and will continue

'til your Spirit has left.

Friendship

Of which you enjoy many,

Some more than others.

Truth lies, in the essence ,

behind the Friendship.

WHAT IS JOY?

Joy is a feeling, a vibration, which lifts the heart. It is pure, it is heavenly, and makes life worth living.
The possibilities of finding Joy, are endless.
Joy is an emotion like Love, it can be felt, it is tangible.
Joy is a healer.
When one brings Joy into their heart, they are healing themselves. Joy is the essence of Life.
The heart needs Joy, it thrives on it.
Joy nourishes us.

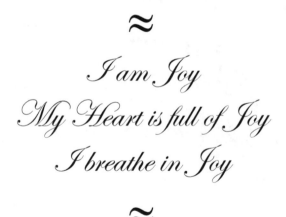

I am Joy

My Heart is full of Joy

I breathe in Joy

The path of Wisdom will bring you Joy.
We bring you Wisdom in abundance.
Be Joyful.

More GEMS!

So many Souls are lost and alone.
How can we reach them and guide them home?
Life is a battlefield, some won, some lost.
Hearts are broken, but who counts the cost?
How much longer will this go on?
When will it stop and man get along?
Lets come together
and make a new start,
to love one another
from heart to heart.

What beauty surrounds us everywhere?
Do we notice, and do we care?
Often missing the simple things
Life has to offer,
That Nature brings.

A Garden tended every day
Will gladden your heart and lift your Soul.
It brings Joy to all and helps soothe the mind.
Quiet times spent, contemplating the magic of nature
Will always bring you inner peace.
Take time to just sit and be still.
Marvel at the designs and colours,
The intricate patterns and delicate fragrances that are all
around us.

WHAT IS AUTOMATIC WRITING?

It is when the hand of Spirit is upon you. We try to convey our thoughts to you, this can be done mind-to-mind or through the medium of hand-writing. We hope to give you works of philosophy as time goes by. We hope you will give us the time needed to bring this about.

There is much work to be done - so much we have to say to you. Creative writing will be channelled, such is the purpose of spiritual communication; we rely on you to be the tool through which we work. Too often, time is the problem we encounter. Too little time is given to the needs of the Spirit.

We draw close to you hoping for attunement, which is necessary before we can begin any form of communication. Words of inspiration, will come to you, as you go about your daily life. We hope that you will pay attention and take the time to put pen to paper. We have faith in you. You are a child of God, first and foremost. Much love comes to you from the source of life. Pray to God, Meditate, whenever you can. We are ever ready to serve you as you serve us.

Bless You

GOD'S CHILDREN

Children everywhere are struggling to be heard.
Open your hearts and minds and *listen* to them.
Let go of *old* values and *old* thinking.
Allow the new energies to flow into your hearts.
Get in touch with your children.
Connect with them on their level.
Take time to hear what *they* are saying.
Release yourselves from rigid thinking.
Be open to new ways and new ideals.
They are the future ~ You can learn from them.
Let *them* into your hearts and minds.
Do not imprison them in the old ways.
They have come into the World to bring change.
Try not to resist what must eventually be.
Comfort and guide the little children.
Difficult times are upon us.
Be guided by them, and be prepared to change.
It is a process that will continue for many years to come.
Children of today are coming in on a higher vibration.
They are more aware of the purpose of life.
Know in your hearts.
All will be well.

ANGELS

Connect with your own Guardian Angel, and allow them
to help you in times of need, they walk by your side,
patiently waiting for permission to help you. We must ask
for their help. We have free-will and they cannot intervene.
Angels guide and protect us, they walk with us, so often
forgotten. Take time to talk to your Guardian Angel, make
that connection by allowing yourself quiet time. Be *still*
and *listen*. Be aware and look for signs and answers to your
prayers. Remember, We are *not* alone!
From Gabriel…

Be true to your own Soul-self within.
Do *not* bow to another's wishes or commands.

Watching over us, every minute of every hour, every day.
They live their lives, helping you to live *your* life, to the best
of your abilities. Bringing *you* the advantages that best help
you, on your return journey to the Godhead, from whence
you came. It is an honour for Angels to serve Mankind,
to be by your side, for they too, are evolving. They are
so filled with Love, even when they present us with
opportunities and challenges to help us learn.. It is always
from a point of Love. That being said, we should not
depend on them to guide our every footstep. We should
listen to our Conscience, and live our lives with integrity.
We should *live* by the example, given by Jesus ~ A True Son
of God.

Bless You.

A MESSAGE FROM THE ANGELS ABOVE

We gather around, as the time draws near, when we shall descend to lower planes, to do God's Will. It is imperative that this be done, for Mankind cannot do it alone. He has much to learn, and still drags his feet. Many are still *stuck* in the mire, unable to access higher minds. In doing so, they could bring about great change on the Earth Plane. It is a plane of Thought, and anything can be created with right-thinking and right-doing. So go about your daily chores with a light heart, and lift yourselves *up* to higher thinking.

Help us to help you.

It is the Will of God that all Man shall return to the source of Life.

We enable you, as you enable one another.

Bless You.

CIRCLES OF LOVE AND LIGHT

Each new Circle that is created, is an opportunity for
The Light to be anchored into the earth. Angelic Beings
have worked hard on our behalf and now Humans are
attempting to do this for themselves. When we gather
together in groups, large or small, and open our hearts and
minds, we enable The Light to be channeled through us, so
bringing The Light into The Earth.
The darkness is being lifted and it's power is now greatly
diminished. Those who stand up and take on the challenge
are known as Light Workers. More and more Circles are
being created, and never before has it been as important,
as it is now, for us to open our hearts and minds to assist
in the raising of the Earth's vibrations. Each Soul that
awakens, adds to The Light and Spiritual weight of the
Planet.
We shall achieve Heaven on Earth, the veil is thinning now,
and the two Worlds are coming together.
Bless you All for spreading Light and Love wherever you go.
All is well, All will be well.

A TRINITY

Mind, Body and Soul ~ One does not work without the others! There must be balance and harmony. Too much attention paid to one or more, causes dis-ease and dis-harmony ~ resulting in illness.
Take care of yourselves and look after *all* aspects of yourself.
   Allow time for your Soul-self; nourish your Mind *and* Body. A little knowledge and a healthy Body, creates a wise Soul.

CHAOS

Out of Chaos, comes Order. This is how it has been since the beginning of time. We should like to express our deep gratitude to those of you who walk the chosen pathway, which we understand can be a difficult one. We Thank you for the work done and the prayers given on behalf of those in need, without them it would not be easy for us. We work for the good of Mankind always.

These are troubled times in which mankind finds himself, brought about by his deeds, his actions, and his thinking. This mess has been caused by greed and corruption. When will Man understand the Truth. You cannot take with you these Earthly goods; material gain is not important. What *is* important, is to strive for perfection, to enhance the Soul through *good* deeds done on Earth.

Spiritual awakening is coming to the fore; so many of you are now aware. Life is changing. Your goals are no longer the same. You must let go of all that you held dear, whether it be material or sentimental. Each of you carries too *much* baggage. There is a clearing of all levels, this can only be achieved if Souls are awakened, and prepared to move on. Those of you who choose this road, will be helped into this *New Age*, but let me say this … This is a once in a lifetime opportunity, it will not come round again. Those left behind *will* struggle for Millennia.

Rise up, and be counted. Take *up* the Sword of Light and
cut yourselves free from the dross, the dark matter that
clings to you. Free yourselves from your self-imposed
prisons. Into the Light you must come. It is the natural
Law, and it *will* be so.

WHAT MAY COME

What may come to each individual Soul, depends on their chosen pathway and their free will. This, of course, can be accepted or refused. All is a matter of Choice. No Soul is forced to do something, or experience that which it does *not* desire to do. Of course, one may 'forget' the purpose of the journey to the Earth, and be confused and angry, when misfortune or ill-health besets them. But we *must* re-member, that all is a result of natural laws ~ Cause and Effect is the root of many situations upon the Earth. One should accept and tolerate, all that is, and know in one's heart, that the Soul's higher self is in control, and knows what is best for us.

Accept with Joy in your hearts, the many trials and difficulties that you encounter, in your lives and *know* that there is a purpose behind all things; that *all* experiences are there to teach and help the soul to grow. Accept, what may come with Love in your hearts, and *know* that all is well, and as it should be. The hardest lessons, are those that benefit us the most.

God Bless You.

HEAL THE EARTH

It is time for Change! No more can the old ways be suffered, where many do not give a moments thought to the consequences, of their behaviour. Excuses made, every Man for himself. What will become of Mankind if he cannot take care of himself, let alone the World he inhabits, which has been entrusted to him. Too much waste in all areas of life. No-one wishes to take responsibility for their actions, always it is the fault of another. When will Man stand up and be counted! Nature has always taken care of Herself, but Mankind's interference has caused imbalance at the very Source of Life, and it will take centuries to put things right.

We know there are many people out there, sitting in small groups and circles. Why not make it an *Earth Circle*? This Planet is in need of help, if she is to ascend. We can help, if we raise our vibrations, time and time again, we *repeat* ourselves! This in turn will help the Earth ~ Our Planet. All it takes is a few moments of our time. Raise our awareness, our consciousness to a higher level ~ be at One with the Light ~ expand and connect with those on the other side of the veil. Assist them in their work. Let us work with them to Spread the Light and Heal the Earth. Visualise Crystal, clear waters; rich, green pastures; a World that is harmonious and trouble-free. See the Peoples of the World coming together, becoming One. All hatred gone. An ending to all wars and fighting between men, replaced by Love and Light.

This was The Plan. Allow yourselves to be Free ~ from petty thinking, greed and corruption. Let yourselves be guided from within. Be gentle. Be kind to one another. Be *good* people! It is only fear that holds you back.

Ascend you shall! It is written, In the Stars!

FOR THOSE WHO SLUMBER STILL

Time has come to remember who you are. What is your purpose here and now. Waken from your dreamless sleep, for it is when you dream that you become real. You walk with closed Hearts and Minds. When you open your Heart and let in the Light, only then can you see the Truth. Take courage in both hands and be who you really are, be not afraid to speak your Truth, even when others turn away with deaf ears. Do not wait for those who surround you, for they will lift their Hearts when they are ready. We all walk the same path, but all at different times. You must step forward now and begin the task that you set yourself. In your Heart you know what to do. Listen to the words and feelings that you receive and act upon them. You are truly a shining Light, as God pours his Love through you.
Bless You.

MORE GEMS

Future generations will be affected by the changes in 2012:
You must all add your spiritual weight to that of
Human consciousness.

Love is the source of All Power. Life cannot function
without the emotion, Love. Human Beings are dependent
upon their emotions, they are able to assess their feelings
through their emotions. When we are not in touch with
our feelings, then our behaviour is affected, and adverse
patterns emerge. When we are able to bring about balance
and control of the emotional body, then our lives run much
more smoothly.

We would choose our words carefully. We are aware of the
predicament in which you find yourselves. Have faith in
what is said: It is of good intention and full of Love and
Light for Mankind. Man has yet to understand the purpose
of life; to enhance the Soul. Together we will do this. In
time Man will see the true wonders of the real World, the
Spirit World, the Realms of Light; first we must prepare
him. We surround you on all dimensions. There is nothing
we do not know that is not known. God knows All.

Too often there is complacency amongst mankind. Too often there is over-indulgence and a lack of will-power. Man underestimates his own abilities.

MEDIUMSHIP - what does it mean to you?

The ability to transfer thoughts telepathically from one plane of Thought to another. We need you as communicators to bring
The Word.

We need channels through which we can communicate our Message to the World. So much needs to be said. So many deaf, dumb and blind to the Truth, the *real* Truth. That which life itself is based upon, the very essence of Life.

In the beginning; at the dawn of time, when *life* began as mere consciousness. An intelligence was born which developed over Millennia, progressing, always moving forward. In time, Man came to The Earth; for it was God's Will to experience all that He knew, all he encompassed. It was an Act of Divine Will. But in Man's mind, there has been a distortion of the Truth. Man's free will has become his own burden, he has served himself before God. Thus he has interfered with Divine Will.

PERCEPTION

As we gather together, to enhance our spirituality, let us know that we are *not* alone in our endeavours. There are those beyond the veil, would seek to bring the two Worlds ever closer. They are Guides and Helpers and often loved ones, who have gone before us to The Other Side. Be assured, there is no physical death, only a passing into a new life, one which we are familiar with. It is a re-birth. A continuation of our Journey. Each One of us has our own pathway; we prepare for each lifetime on the Earth. We make the decisions before we return, it is our own free will which brings us here time after time, to experience the many facets of life. It is so easy for us to accept all the good things we do; why can we not see and understand the need to also experience the opposite? It is *not* bad, or wrong. It is our beliefs we must change. Our reality is only what we believe it to be, or how we perceive it to be. Each one of us would have a different reality of the same situation, for it is *how* we perceive what is around us, that gives us our realities. Greater awareness is coming to Mankind, and with this, an awakening to Higher Consciousness.

JOURNEY OF THE FOOL

The Journey of the Fool is a precarious one, as he steps forward one foot in front of the other, until he reaches the point of no return. Then must he take a giant step forward, a blind leap of faith. This you must do; the outcome is known - it has been planned like the part in a play, now it must be staged. You know this is so, and you have the faith.

Remember who you are!

We say this time and time again.

You are awesome in God's eyes. You are magnificent. You have earned your passage. There is always work to be done. You have the Love and support of many from beyond the veil.

Time draws near when all will be revealed. Choirs of Angels shall be heard.

NEW ENERGIES FOR THE NEW AGE

It has begun. The change is upon us. And things are moving forward. Nothing can stop this perpetual motion, as old energies dissipate. The new higher vibrations on which the Earth is moving up, as she ascends, will bring Light. It has been said, *Where there is darkness, there will be Light.* It has begun, and it shall be so.

JOURNEYS OF THE SOUL

Each one individual and tailor-made for the Soul
concerned. Each waking moment is spent remembering
the Soul-purpose and trying to achieve the personal goal set
by the Spirit before it's re-birth into the Earth.
Many Planets are teeming with Life, but for Humans it
is essential to return to Earth, the Planet of Free Will, to
progress onward and upward. Nowhere is there another
Plane of existence which can remedy the needs of the Soul,
as well as Planet Earth.

  Time and time again, we return to master and perfect the
  Soul, as it journeys back to the beginning of Life, to the
  Creator, the Source of All Life: to be absorbed back into
  the very energy that created it. The Light will consume
  the darkness, and Life will begin again. It will create yet
  another cycle of life, only to repeat it again and again.

THE BIRTH OF A CHILD

There is nothing greater than the Miracle of Life, as a new Young Soul enters the Earth Plane.. It is with great sadness, as it prepares for it's difficult Journey ahead, leaving loved-ones behind. Having chosen the theme and the experiences it will undergo, the right circumstances must prevail, for every detail is looked at most carefully. Infinite possibilities exist and nothing is left to chance. We can make choices, knowing we must live the consequences. We must take responsibility for ourselves. All this, and much more, a Soul knows and will take many lifetimes to remember.

WORDS FOR THE LITTLE CHILDREN

Listen to those around you, who have gone before you.
Know that they have already walked the very path that you
now tread, with trepidation and fear. Let go of the fear,
for it will not advance you on your Journey. Seek only the
good in Life and in others. Stay in the Light at all times.
You say, *How do I know*?
 Listen and you will be guided, by those around you; those
that walk with you: always let Love be your guide. Love is
the anchor, it is the cornerstone of Life. Always has been
and always will be. This is life acceptance. This is the key
to Happiness. You may not always understand, but there
is a Divine Purpose. All things are as they are meant to be.
You are living in the *Now.* You cannot remember what has
gone before. Trust in the Divine Plan of God Almighty.
You are His Children, and he loves you.

A MESSAGE FROM THE OTHER SIDE

People are far too concerned with the material world.
Always they neglect their spiritual bodies.
In the not too distant future, a stark reminder will be given.
Did I, The Son Of God, not set an example, of how to live one's life! Forgotten by so many, The Purpose of Life, and the Journeys the Soul has already forged through the Planes of Life. Great tragedies and difficulties have been overcome, only to be buried under greed and corruption, and self-satisfaction.
What of Morals? And Kindness to others!

A Soul's true desire

is to shed the layers,

Until it is pure light

and is able to be absorbed into

The One, The Whole,

The All that is God.

Each sojourn on the Earth

enables the Soul to grow

and shed the covering,

revealing the True Self.

FROM LAO ~ A FRIEND IN SPIRIT

Almighty God, Father in Heaven
Looks down upon His children,
With such Love in His Heart.
Great Joy he feels for you,
Each of you,
His Blessed Children.
Peace be with you.
Love Divine is within each of you,
And it shall shine forth
To guide the way for those
who endeavour to seek
The Light of the New Energy
That comes to the Earth.
Blessings to all those upon the Earth, who are struggling to
maintain their chosen pathway upon the Earth plane. It is
difficult, it was never going to be easy. You were aware of
that before you came. You must try to remember the many
choices and decisions you made, to enable you to progress,
further along the spiritual pathway that leads you back
home, back to Divine Source from which you have come.
You have travelled this way before, for many millennia, and
will continue to do so.

BELOVED SON OF GOD

What perils have beset Mankind, and yet he continues to blindly follow the herd. The folly of Humankind has been his downfall. It was made clear in the beginning, and yet Man in his fear and ignorance, has hidden the Truth. But the Truth shall be recognised and all that is false shall be torn asunder. The promise that the Kingdom of Heaven shall be upon the Earth, *will* come to be, for it is My Father's Will. The Light shall overcome the darkness. It is known. It has been spoken. It shall come to pass.

Blessed are they that follow the Way of the Lord, for it leads to the Kingdom of God.

Come unto Me, for I am my Father's Keeper.

It is through me, that each Soul shall return.

I am the Shepherd, and all lambs of God shall repent and Ascend unto Heaven. Even the stray ones shall return to the fold. God awaits His Children.

I Am, The Son of God. Follow Me into The Kingdom of Heaven, to our Heavenly Father. Who forgives us all our sins, for He loves all his Children dearly.

THE MAGNIFICENCE OF MOTHER EARTH

The beauty that is all around us must never be taken for granted, for Nature is finely tuned. Man has interfered, and there now exists imbalance. A tiny seed that grows and blooms into an exquisite flower, with delicate perfume, is a part of the same Energy of Nature that brings us a gentle breeze on a summer's day, that can become a violent, destructive force, a hurricane or tornado.
On the surface, we can see the beauty of majestic mountains, and yet, far below the Earth's crust, a river of molten lava flows, seeking out an avenue, through which to pour onto the surface of the beautiful world above.
On one side of Nature, we have peace and tranquillity, and on the opposite, storms which wreak havoc and death upon us.

The World must retain balance, and we must work towards restoring harmony. The Earth is multi-layered, and Mankind has a duty to respect the awesome power of Nature, which has the ability to nurture the Human Race, or destroy us.

WALK, NOT ALONE.

Walk not with your face to the ground. Open your eyes
~ see what is really around you, not what you want to see.
Try not to control situations, let them flow. Do *not* fight
against life, for there is purpose, rhyme and reason for all
that happens. For *nothing* happens without reason. There
is a rhythm that flows. Go with that natural flow, and see
how life falls into place. Do the right thing, always, and see
how your own life's purpose will unfold.
Be kind to others. Be compassionate. Do not judge, for
you know not the story of another's life. You see only one
page at a time, you do not ever read the whole book. Only
God, the Great White Spirit, knows all. Each of you create
your own life story, from beginning to end.

Such a long time now.
Many years since I walked the Earth.
So many Souls are struggling.
Great Awakening coming to those who choose to listen, to
walk their chosen pathway, as I am walking mine. I walk
alongside many, guiding their footsteps, holding them
when they falter.
So much work to do, to bring Humankind to a level of
vibration where we can communicate with ease. So many
refuse to listen. They hear us, but they do not listen.
How many of you listen to the natural sounds of the World
in which you live: *Really* listen - to the Songs of the Birds in
the Sky that call to you; the sound of the Rain as it cleanses;
even the melody of the babbling brook, or the Crashing of
the Waves, or the Wind in your Face , as it caresses you?
Feel the Sun upon your Skin. Let it warm you. Let it's
Light awaken you. Lift up your Heads and Lift your
Hearts.

A HEAVENLY HAND FOR HUMANKIND

Life is precious, never more so than at this time. Man has been on the Earth for aeon, alone and feeling separated from Heavenly Realms. Time is upon us now, when energies are finer, and the veil of unconsciousness is thinning. Man is now succeeding in raising his vibrations and is becoming aware of his Higher Consciousness, which is allowing access to higher states of mind.

GRATITUDE

So many people sail through life without a single thought towards another, taking whatever comes their way, but never thinking to give *Thanks* to whomever or whatever did the giving. It is time that Man stopped in his tracks, and turned things around!

Let us give to others rather than receive.

Ask, 'What can *I* do for someone else today?'

Be thankful for *all* the help received.

Do something good for someone else, no matter whether it is big or small.

Think only of others - *How* will your actions affect those around you.

Give of yourself and not just material things.

Make time to change just one small thing.

Realise *everything* you do and say can affect another - good or bad.

Make an effort to be honest, kind and caring.

CONTEMPLATION

It is good to sit and think, to find quiet time to reflect on situations around us. Sometimes we act in haste, and have regrets afterwards. Too little time is spent quietly contemplating life as we see it and feel it. Try to focus on the problem in hand. Do not let the mind wander, but stay focused, and concentrate on the matter you wish to find a solution to. You will find as time goes by, this will become easier to do. Reflect on a situation if you are not comfortable with it. Do not be afraid to speak the Truth, even if you know it is not what others wish to hear. Too often, people turn a deaf ear to the Truth, allowing the ego to take control, and not accepting responsibility for their own actions. Be prepared to be criticised, but stand your ground and always speak the Truth, with Honesty and Integrity.

JEWEL OF THE COSMOS

Planet Earth, suspended within it's own Universe, a
sparkling Jewel, a rare commodity; specialised Journeys
for Humankind; a Sojourn like no other, is available on
your Planet. A Sea of Emotions in which to learn the finer
lessons in life. Journeys planned for the individual and
tailor-made, where Life can be experienced through many
different facets.

The Following were received at precisely 11:11 pm.
CHANGES

It is time for Change! For the old energies are dissipating
to make room for higher frequencies. Generosity of Spirit
is sadly lacking in your World, and there is a great need for
the spiritual upliftment of many Souls at this time. Many
are confused. They sense the coming changes, but are
unsure of what direction to take.

We advise to look inward to the Self for guidance. Ask, and
it shall be given. Take a quiet moment to reflect inwardly,
and sense the direction that is needed to be taken.

We walk with you, we guide your every move and hear your
thoughts. Nothing is said or done that is not known. All is
seen and all is heard. All is well.

Take Heart, Children of the Earth, All is not lost.

A True Awakening is Coming.

Those who are prepared will be blessed.

Freedom from the mind is achieved by going within, and
being still, as in meditation. You have the power to take
control. One must be in control. Listen and Observe. The
importance of maintaining balance, makes it possible to
achieve the Enlightenment you seek.

Be *aware* at all times. Be conscious of a *higher self* within.
And we say again. *Wake up!*

11:11 ~ 27.04.2009
THE TRUTH

My Friends on Earth, we welcome this opportunity to
communicate with *you*.

Far be it for us to dictate to you, we would rather you
would listen to the Truth, and accept that which is of use
to you at this given time. What you may accept today, as
Truth, may indeed change in the future. Be aware of this.
Never accept all that you receive as gospel, but only that
which is reality for you at that time. This of course, may
change, as I have said before. Your Truth may or may not be
the same as another.

We are each walking our own individual pathways, whilst
treading the road of life on Earth. We experience what we
need as individuals, to further our own personal growth.
This is the Soul-Purpose of Life in the Earth. To strip away
the outer layers, to reach the Golden Nugget within - that is
the Heart Centre, the very Essence of your spiritual Being.
Release all fears, and transmute the dense energies into Pure
Light. This is done with unconditional Love. Love is the
Source of All Life. It is where you have come from and
where you shall return. The Godhead is Pure untainted
Love.

11:11 ~ 29.04.2009
COUNCIL of NINE

We are the Elder Brethren who preside over all Spiritual matters on the Earth. We communicate to your Guides and Helpers, and they in turn will communicate with you. This is done with the power of thought transference, we do not hold meetings with those on lower vibrational planes. This is not possible. It would be of great discomfort for an individual Soul. Although we can lower our vibrations, if so desired, to achieve a mission.

Fear not for the Planet Earth, All is as it should be. And all is in accordance with God's Will, which is of course, the Universal Mind. 11:11 will be made clear at the precise *moment* in time. We are highly evolved Souls who have long since journeyed to the Earth. It is the destiny of all Souls to return from whence they came, back to the Source of All Life.

11:11 ~ 01.05.2009
A WONDER TO BEHOLD

Earth is indeed a wonder to behold. Held in great esteem
by the many Solar Systems of the Universe. We watch with
trepidation, as Humankind takes on the responsibility of
raising the vibrations of the Earth, to enable her ascension,
to take her rightful place. Man must overcome the greed
and ignorance that is rife on your Planet. Only then will
Human consciousness be raised, to a level that can benefit
those of you, who have chosen to assist with this difficult
task. It is now quite feasible, and we still assist you, as
much as we are able. You are not alone at any time. All
eyes are upon you. For our future rests on the outcome of
Planet Earth.
The Earth is truly a place of beauty for all to enjoy. It is
God's creation, and is seen from Heaven ~ all aglow. There
are mountains high-capped with snow, and lush green
valleys down below. Endless blue skies, and oceans cover
her surface. Seeds germinate deep in the ground, and burst
forth reaching for the sunlight, as they strive to grow. Many
to bear fruit and others to flower, in the Glory of God.
Planet Earth is home to millions of animals and birds, alike.
We ask you to take *better* care of *her*.

11:11 ~ 04.06.2009
What Can You Tell Me About 2012?

It will be a time of great change and upheaval. Many souls will have already returned home. Those who remain, have made the choice to be on the Earth, and help others make the transition from the *old* to *The New*.

There will be many disasters, leading up to 2012, to facilitate this mass-exodus. It has begun. Great Changes are taking place, and new World Leaders are emerging. America and England will lead the way and show the rest of the world, by example. Governments will reform. Greed and corruption will eventually be wiped out. There is no room for this selfish thinking in the future.

All will be well.

Discoveries will be made which will turn the scientific world on it's head. There will be new thinking, as The Truth is spread. Brotherhood of Man is imminent. Faith and Trust will strengthen all four corners of the World. Barriers will crumble, along with boundaries and borders. It has been announced to The World, that The *End is near*, that Armageddon is upon us. What poppycock, I say!

Surely Changes are coming. Man must be made to realise, he alone is responsible for all the problems he encounters. It is his own doing and the result of centuries of rape and pillage of Mother Earth.

Take. Take. Take! *That* is the fault of Man!

Greed and corruption is rife, and never before has there been a greater need for Human-kind to take stock, and stand up and be counted.

Man must accept responsibility and make amends for *all* wrong-doing. It is not too late, but so many Humans still have their heads buried in the sand, so to speak!
What can we do, they cry: and they *do* nothing!
Many adding to the problems with their very behaviour.
We say *again*, to you, help is at hand. Planet Earth shall be saved.. The veil has thinned to such a degree, we are able to move from one Plane of Life to another. It is not a trick.
Many of us walk amongst you. When the time is right, and 2012 will soon be upon us, we shall assist you.
It is your destiny, and the Earth shall ascend to higher vibrations. Soon you shall all acknowledge us, for we shall be seen. Angels will come in their thousands, to aid The Earth in her promised ascension, where she shall take her rightful place. Peace be with you, Child of Light.

Bless you.

THE SPOKEN WORD

Many, many words have been channelled and written over the years, but the World in which you live is changing, and there is much to be said, to prepare those Souls who remain on the Earth during this period of transition. We are gladly joining forces, and there are Souls on this side of life, who are indeed searching for suitable Channels, through which they can work and bring forth new ideas and new thinking, that are relevant to the new energies of this time.

We support you in all that you do, and guide you to make right decisions, which will enable you to progress to the best of your ability.

Fear not, My Child, your hard work will come to fruition. You are never idle and we work continuously in preparation for future goals that have been set. I am with you daily.

THE WHITE BROTHERHOOD

Aeon of time have passed since Man began his descent
to the Realms of the Earth plane, steadily progressing
forward with each Journey taken: the Soul taking on new
experiences, challenges, and ever more difficult tasks, to
express itself, so that the Godhead ~ the all-powerful, all-
knowing, Holy Spirit ~ which we all strive to ascend to ~
may know, may experience also, the Physical.
The trials and tribulations of Life on Earth serve a purpose.
Through these happenings, the Soul is perfecting him
or herself. The many lifetimes vary according to each
individual Soul-part, which in turn is part of a Soul-group/
family.

We who are members of The White Brotherhood have
completed our time of learning on the Earth and have
ascended to higher Planes of Life, where we exist for
the good of Mankind - our Soul-Purpose being that of
enhancing those Souls who are striving, to fulfil their desire
to evolve to higher vibrations of existence.

What Will Happen in 2012?

Many Souls will return home, one way or another, as we have said before. What appear to you as *disasters* are merely a way for Group Souls to return to The Light. Those of you who have chosen to remain, will work to raise the vibrations of Mankind to a higher level, so that the two worlds may unite once more. Much help will be given, as it is already under way and huge progress has been made. Many Souls are part of this tremendous effort, and it will be successful, it can only be so. Those who have not touched the Earth for a very long time, will do so once again, for the Earth's vibration will be raised, and this will again be possible. The Earth Plane has been through a very dark period indeed, and still has some way to go. She is not *out of the woods* yet, as you say. We are doing our utmost to assist you all in every way. Consciousness is already improving greatly, for many Souls, but the work must go on to reach the goals necessary, for the Quantum Leap to manifest itself upon the minds of Mankind - who has yet to be liberated.

Angels and Hosts of Light Beings are among you this very day. They reach out to you with Love and we *know* that you recognise them from within.

God Bless you children of The Light

Freedom will come to you.

In 2012

We tell you there is a great need for Souls to evolve. They
must take a look at themselves and their way of life as
individuals; How can they improve and become more
aware: How can they develop their spirituality?
Open their Hearts and become One with The Divine.
Connect with their Souls, their Higher Selves.

    2012 will help all those who wish to help themselves. It
will no longer be possible to live in ignorance. The right
path will be shown to all and efforts must be made by
Mankind as a whole.

THE ESSENCE OF JOY

Joy is the essence of All Life. It must flow in and out. It is
the spiritual force which flows through the heart. Without
Joy, we would close our hearts to the spiritual Love available
to us. Open your heart. Bring Joy into your Life.

Joy! Joy! Joy! - to the world!
We are filled with Joy when you sit in the quiet, so that we
may draw close to you.
You need more Joy in your Life.
Stop letting others control your days!

A Shining Light even when you stand out from others, you
are never alone.
The One is always a part of The Whole.
Inner beauty shines forth, even if it cannot be seen with
physical eyes What we see is far greater.
                    We see the whole picture.

LIFE

The berries on the tree represent the Cycle of Life.
New growth is *re-birth!*
Just as the humans do, the Soul re-incarnates, to enjoy or
experience a period of re-growth.
It is much the same, whilst a plant lies dormant, to prepare
for new growth, on a much grander scale, the Soul returns
to the homeland to rest a while and prepare for a new life
upon the Earth, hence the term *death*.
Of course there is no such thing as *death*.
It is an experience for the purpose of the Soul to move on.
It is merely the shedding of a cloak, or a skin, to reveal a
new cloak of many colours. Each time the Soul returns, it
is expressing itself.

The True Self is not visible, and as the Soul grows in
experience, it no longer requires a vehicle to enter into
dense matter. It is able to continue it's Journey into the
Light without returning to the Physical.

LOST IN TIME

What time is wasted as you go about your daily lives, totally
immersed in *things* that have no importance.
What a total waste of time!
Do you know how *precious* Time is?
How can you not know, that Time does not stand still! It is
in essence, a continual motion.
The clock ticks upon the wall. You watch time go by, and
live your lives by the face on the clock.
Be still a while, and stand in *The Now*.
Be *aware* of the space around you: for does not *time* exist
on all levels - past, present and future.
All are one and the same.
Do not wait for another *time* to do what you must do.
                    Live in the *Now*.

WORDS OF UPLIFTMENT FOR THE DOWNHEARTED

Cherish the Life you have been given; look within for the answers to the questions you ask daily. For *you* already know the answers. Lift the veil, and The Truth will reveal itself.

Do not be dishonest with yourself. All Beings know in *their* heart *their* true feelings.

Do not mask the Truth with sympathy for others. Apathy serves only to hinder one's growth.

Be True to your Self ~ do not wallow in self-pity, for you yourself have created the very conditions that surround you. No other has done this.

You are living your own Truth, and creating the reality daily, with your thoughts and emotions. Only *you* have the power to change what *you* have set in motion. The natural laws by which we all live cannot be altered in any way.

The Laws of Cause and Effect, and Action and Re-action, which affect *troubled* Mankind, are constantly in motion, and no matter how much *he* tries to lay the blame at God's feet, *he*, in essence, has created the very conditions which threaten *his* existence.

We are at hand, and do all within our power, to help and assist mankind. The tide is turning; we shall succeed.

God Be With You.

AWAKENING THE SOUL

We come to the Earth as part of our lessons in life. We
journey here many times, to experience many different life
situations, through difficult circumstances. Each lifetime
is planned by our Higher Self, with assistance from our
Guides and Helpers. We choose who we will return with,
often within the same group of Souls to grow.
We are like unpolished Diamonds, and each Journey to the
Earth, enables us to polish and perfect, yet another facet
of ourselves. The purpose of Life is to grow and mature in
Mind, Body and Soul. After many Sojourns to the Earth,
we will be ready to awaken the Soul, while still in the Earth.
This can be a trying time for the Human and is not always
accomplished. It takes discipline and courage to awaken
the Soul, and bring harmony and balance to the Mind and
Body. Often it will take repeated attempts to complete the
tasks we set ourselves. Once awakened, the Soul desires
to rise, and eventually to ascend to Higher Realms of
Consciousness, where it will continue to progress onward
and upward, until it is absorbed into the source of All Life.
At-one-ment with God, the Journey complete.

LOVE AND LIGHT

We come in Love and Light. Fear not. Love will conquer all fear. Love will manifest in many different forms upon the Earth Planes in the near future. Some will recognise these subtle changes, but many are blind and do not see. Changes will come gradually, and life will continue to ebb and flow.

Those of you who are torch-bearers, also known as Light Workers, will know these changes.

New energies will be made manifest on the Earth through those Souls who have chosen to do this work.

Each of you has a role to play. Work has already begun. The aim of which is to unite Mankind with his Soul-body, his Body of Light.

Vibrational energy will take Mankind forward on his Journey back to the Source. Become aware of the change of energy in the Earth. The very *vibrations* that are the *foundations*, are evolving.

PALETTE Of An ARTIST

Filled with the base colours, but always the possibilities of many variations, one colour flows into another, creating new colours all the time, endless shades of colour. So is Life.

This way or that way, it does not matter which pathway one chooses, for they all lead to the same. We are all journeying in the same direction, returning to the same point from which we began our incredible journey, many, many aeon of time ago.

COLOURS OF THE LIGHT

Red ~   Energy and Strength. Gives encouragement to go on. Courage.

Orange ~   Uplifting, Vitality and Confidence ~ fills us with Joy and Happiness.

Yellow ~   Connects us with the Universal Mind, bringing Knowledge and Wisdom. Learning.

Green ~   The colour of Nature, One-ness. New Beginnings. Harmony and Balance ~ Health.

Turquoise ~   New Heart Centre., linking with Higher Soul Energies. Lighter Vibrations.

Blue ~   Healing and Calming. It teaches Trust. The Centre of Communication ~ Faith.

Indigo ~   Gives us Power of spiritual Knowledge. Links to our Higher Minds. Third Eye, Clairvoyance.

Violet ~   The Colour of True Spiritual Inspiration and One-ness with All That Is ~ Truth and Light.

THE ART OF SCIENCE

The Art of Science is quite literally, the study of the human mind. Breaking down boundaries which create limited thinking. The process has been slow and laborious. Man began his journey hundreds of years ago. Studying the ways of Mankind and what caused him to behave in certain ways. What was the thinking behind the action?
The Human Mind is awesome, and it possesses the power to create anything known to Man. Science will come full circle. What was discovered centuries ago, and kept hidden, will be exposed, and accepted as a *breakthrough* in modern science.

CHAKRAS

The chakras are a very complex subject. At the beginning, it all seems quite simple but as you delve deeper you are struck by the complexity. Trying to understand them whilst on the Earth Plane is difficult, as you cannot comprehend the depth of the subject, especially when linking with the higher levels.

MESSAGE FOR HUMANITY

Time is running out for you all.
Take time out to be still, or all will be lost to you.
Listen, be still, go within; seek solace and peace.
Do not fret and stress, forget the material *wants*.
As you connect with your Soul, all else falls into place.
Meditate for a few moments at a time.
Do this daily and increase the time spent meditating, as you improve.
Your life is what you make it.

CHANGES

Changes are brought about by reflection, by taking a closer look at what has been said and done, shining a light on the dark recesses of the mind. By bringing Truth and Honesty into everything we do and say. Searching within and asking ourselves what we may do better or how should we do things next time, when a difficult lesson has been learned. Always, Love will bring change, if a situation is intolerable. It is the Quest of each Soul to learn, Unconditional Love for all.
Bless You.

REFLECTIONS

Let us reflect on the purpose of meditation and the advantages of being still and allowing our Guides to draw close, which is only possible if we can still the chattering mind and bring our bodies to a state of stillness.

Once we are relaxed , then we are able to sense the finer vibrations that surround us, which during the course of a normal day, we are not aware of.

The breath should be the focal point and you should try to remain aware of each in-ward breath and each out-ward breath, and not drift off into a state of semi-sleep.

It is no longer necessary to go off into a deep trance like state of meditation; we are able to communicate and influence your minds whilst you are purely still and quiet.

The purpose of meditation is to re-connect with the Higher Self and those who inhabit the higher planes of consciousness.

Our minds have many levels and it is important to only access the level to which we are attuned. Generally those who are wishing to communicate are aware of the level of vibration on which you are able to work, but occasionally in their haste and excitement, they may try and push forward, which can create an imbalance and distort the energies, resulting in physical discomfort. When this occurs it is necessary for you to withdraw, asking the Spirit Being involved to step back. Remember, they need your permission, and it should always be a two-way agreement. The purpose being for your enhancement and Soul growth.

TWO FEATHERS

What a pleasure to work with you this evening my friend,
such a lovely Light - Thank you.

The opportunity to speak where it will be heard and
understood is rare indeed. We need the Light as well as you
do.

It is a challenge indeed to bring the Two Worlds together,
but succeed we must. The Planet Earth is in great need
at this time. We will return. We should not have left the
Earth when we did, we were before our time.

We were a civilised people in an un-civilised part of the
World. We made many mistakes of course, but our truths
will surface. They have survived, the time past. It is locked
into the memories of those who know. Enlightenment
is coming to the lower planes where you exist. A Great
Awakening indeed.

      Bless You, I will speak to you again.

JOURNEY OF THE SOUL

There is a flow and pattern to the Journey of the Soul. All is done in accordance with the wishes of the Soul, the greater part of ourselves. All is known, and each incarnation will be planned so that the Soul will benefit and reach the desired goal, through the challenges and circumstances chosen to be experienced in the Earth. Do not question, for your Higher Self knows best, and is working from a higher perspective. Go with the Flow of Life, resistance is futile. Acceptance and co-operation is the key to success. Be creative, set yourself new targets, always pushing forward and expressing yourself, in as many different forms as possible.

You have latent talents, experiment and bring out the best *in you*. You can be all things, there are no limitations, only those you impose on yourselves.

Life on Earth is a unique opportunity for growth of the Soul, but it is often hampered by *fear*. Reluctance to change stems from *fear*, release yourselves. Let Go, *And Let God*, is a wonderful expression. Do it!

Bless You.

PRAYERFUL THOUGHT

Limit yourself to ungoverned thinking, discipline your minds.

Do not allow selfish and sabotaging thoughts.

Keep your mind free from all negative thinking, and allow your mind to blossom and grow with right-thinking and positivity.

Free your minds from pre-conceived ideas, do not fill your minds with others' beliefs.

Accept only that *which you have reasoned with,* and can accept as Truth.

Always think clearly, concisely, and never let your mind be anything less than Love and Light.

Be liberal in your search for Spirituality, seek the Truth, for the Truth will set you free from the bonds of Earth. You have a choice - remain where you are, or move onward and upward.

This is your ultimate goal.

Why waste precious time? Face your fears and you shall experience Freedom. Your purpose on Earth is to accomplish all that you set up for yourselves, which will eventually result in Soul-growth.

Accept responsibility for Who and What you are.

Bless You.

A NEW ERA

It is the dawn of a New Era upon the Earth, such as, has never been experienced before. After the Great Flood ~ Life began anew. Great changes were set in motion and Man began his Journey of ascent. Natural Laws were adhered to, and the process of rising back up to the Godhead began. Compensation and Retribution became the order of the day, and all deeds were met with Karmic reward and dept. Each Soul is responsible for it's own Self and none other. Take personal responsibility for your actions, and know there is nothing a Soul can do that is not known to God. All is seen, and all is heard. All is held in the Akashic Records.

Many Souls have yet to grasp this, and understand, that even their thoughts are held in the Ether and become solid in Matter.

We in Spirit, (dis-carnate Souls) try to aid and assist those on the Earth, but we cannot intervene against natural laws. We can only respond when asked for help, and permission is given, by the higher Self, which is the greater part of the Soul. Many Masters have returned to the Earth to live by example and show Humankind the Way. Life is an experience, an opportunity for Soul growth, and as such it can be challenging. Each Soul plans and prepares each Sojourn upon the Earth, to maximise it's growth and potential.

Re-connect with the Source, the Creator of All Life. Search within for the answers. When, you feel lost, alone, confused or frightened, find the peace and harmony you desire by becoming still; meditate daily: remember you are Spirit, and are having a Human experience. You are not alone from the moment you enter the world until *death*, which is, in fact, your re-birth. Your Journey complete, you return to the Spirit World, where you will evaluate your Life, and the decisions made - how they have affected your progress.

Life is about Choice and Free Will, one's actions bring about *re*-action, the natural Law of Cause and Effect comes into play.

We all have Free Will, but we must enjoy or suffer, the consequences of *our* actions. Make the most of Life on Earth. It is a unique experience and has been created especially for all of us, we are all God's Children.

Live your lives with Love, and add to the Light of your Soul, which will aid your ascension. Our Planet has a Soul Energy and is evolving. We can help by increasing our *own* Light. Listen to the guidance of the Spirit within. Open your Hearts and Minds and allow Love and Divine Inspiration to *flow*.

Bless You.

RAINBOW OF LOVE

The Colours of the Rainbow are the colours of the vibrations of life, each of you journey through the many layers of colour, each one a different level of Light.

You are now reaching higher levels; let the Light flow through you. Fill your Beings with the Light. We will draw closer to you as time goes by, nearing the time when the Light will break through the dense energy and vibrations of the Earth Plane.

LIFE AND DEATH

Beyond earthly death, there is Life. Death is merely a stage the Soul passes through to enable it to leave the Physical Plane. We survive this transition, and return to Higher Realms of Consciousness, where we exist in Spirit. When a Soul comes to the Earth, it becomes *incarnate.* On it's return, it is then discarnate. Life is Infinite. There is only Life after life. Death is not an ending, but a continuation. When it is *time* for a Soul to return, then it must pass back into Spirit, and this can only be achieved through earthly death. Do not fear *death* as you call it. It is your re-birth into the World of spirit, a Realm of Light from where you came.

All those who have gone before you are continuing their lives, they are *home* once more, with Loved Ones. There is no *death*, only Life.

We are able to communicate through those on Earth known as *Mediums* because they are tuned into higher vibrations. Every Human has this ability and soon all will be made easier, by the Quantum Shift in Consciousness. Do not fear *Spirit*, it is your true form.

Death is a portal ~ back into Life: a short journey indeed! So why do you fear death? It is in actual fact re-birth into Spirit.

As you enter into the Earth Planes, you are separated from the greater part of your Soul. It is necessary, for the mind would become unbalanced if it could recall past-life memories.

Access to the God-energy is through stillness - the Art of Meditation.

When Man connects with his God-energy within, then he is able to relinquish *fear*, and replace it with Faith and

Trust.
Death is merely an Ending and a Beginning.

ELEMENTALS

We gather around you, always ready and willing to assist
you.
Spare us a thought during your busy days.
Send us a little Light and Love.
Open your Hearts and Minds; allow yourselves to *believe*
in us, for we truly exist. We are as *rear* as you are, and are
journeying alongside you, we just exist on another plane of
life. If you truly *believe* in Faeries, then you may glimpse
us if you take the time to be still. The Will 'O The Wisp
fleetingly passes you by. The gnomes tapping their feet
impatiently, as they sit waiting to be noticed. Have you
ever seen the many Faerie, as they tend the garden in the
early morning dew? A Faerie Ring in the grass is the only
sign left behind. A sudden movement in the corner of your
eye, but it is a World hidden from Humans. A realm of
mystery and magic, soon to be revealed to those with vision
and a song in their heart. Tune in to finer vibrations, to
catch a glimpse of Faerie Folk and Angelic Beings.

FAERIE FOLK

Misunderstood, but we Elementals live for the Humans.
It is our destiny to travel with you, as you journey onward
and upward. We aid the Human in the Earth, bringing
you Love of a higher vibration. Transformation is the
key to Enlightenment and can only be achieved with
Spiritual awakening of the Soul that lies within. We work
continuously to raise the energies of all living things. We
aid Mankind on all levels, expecting nothing in return but

Love.

BLESSINGS

Each one of you is showered with Blessings. Often the most difficult challenges are truly a blessing in disguise. Look around you and truly see what surrounds you day to day. The Glory of God is everywhere ~ in the Beauty of Nature, the Animal Kingdom, in the Smile of a Stranger as they pass you by, in the Light that shines in a Childs eyes, within the stillness to be found in your Heart. *Count your Blessings* and remember to give *Thanks* daily.
Bless You.

WORDS FOR THE LIVING

Welcome from the World of Light, from all those who have gone before. We wait in the wings, as you continue with your journey, on the lower Astral Planes, including the Earth Plane. So much has gone awry. Selfishness and lack of compassion has been the source of Mankind's fall. When will he learn, Centuries later, still making the same mistakes; refusing to accept responsibility for his actions, always ready to point a finger at another. Oh What Shame! Think of others, put their needs before your own ~ then we can turn things around.

WHAT LIES WITHIN

A Place of such Peace, it is unintelligible to the Human mind. Fear not this space within, it is not a void, but a limitless place, so full of Love. Allow yourselves to explore this Infinite Light, that goes beyond all Time and Space. It feels like *home,* a child within it's mothers womb, safe and secure. Your true self lies here ~ protected and nurtured, your heart-self. Once you re-connect with your true self within, your Divine Light will shine more brightly.

Bless You.

REACHING BEYOND

A difficult task, but once it is accomplished, the desire
to return again and again is overwhelming. A feeling of
peace and serenity not found in the physical world, a place
that cannot be described, and yet it is known to Souls. It
lies beyond the veil. So close, yet unreachable, A state of
meditation is required, where your vibrations have been
raised, enabling you to access this sought-after realm of
consciousness.
Reaching Beyond is the destiny of Humankind.

OUTCOMES

Why do we not tell your fortunes and the future of the
Planet Earth.
Because of Choice!
God gave Man, Free Will, and as has been said, many times
before, there exist endless possibilities. We can foresee
different Outcomes, and we influence the minds of Man,
wherever and whenever possible.
But we *repeat* - there is no set Outcome!
There is Ascension, for all Beings of Light,
Humanity must return "en masse" to The source,
The Creator, The Universe ~ God!

It is the purpose of Life, for all aspects of the Godhead to
experience, to know itself. We are all one. All is a part of
the Cosmic Mind. All things are connected. All Beings
seek At-one-ment with God, the Source of All Life, The
Light ~ Consciousness.

PATHWAY OF LIGHT

It lies ahead of you, straight as an arrow, but so often we refuse to step upon it, usually from a lack of knowledge or a feeling of fear. But truly we say to you, *The Pathway of Light* is a journey all Souls must eventually walk. It is the Way Home.

Once your feet are firmly planted upon it, you will see the signs and recognise the direction which you need to take. Always following the heart, which is guided by your Soul. Wandering from your chosen pathway will only serve to lengthen your journey, and may bring you false hopes and desires.

We must always return, to move forward, there is no shortcut! Rewards are received for deeds done, but we must all live the consequences of our thoughts and actions.

Go Within for true guidance, for your Soul knows what is best, another does not know your journey. Give generously of yourselves, but never force your will upon another.

What you see as *help* may actually *hinder* their progress. Always live with Love and Kindness to others, and you will reap the benefits.

TROUBLED TIMES

Let us reflect on the troubles of the World, too much emphasis is given to material gain, so many Humans have forgotten their purpose, the reason they returned to Earth. Bring back the simple things in Life. The importance of family values and truth. We must take better care of our bodies and recognise the Spirit within. Fill our minds with only that which will enhance us.

Man has begun to awaken, the *new* Era is upon him. Slowly over time, change will become apparent as we evolve into Spiritual Beings. As we raise our consciousness, we naturally lift our vibrations, enabling us to ascend spiritually. This is the Soul Purpose of Life and as each individual Soul reaches ascension, it returns to the Godhead from which it came.

Humankind *must* learn Unconditional Love, but first Man must Love and Honour himself. One cannot Love another if they have not found At-One-Ment with the Divine Self within.

NEW BEGINNINGS

What is Life?

Should we not consider the purpose of being born as Humans? What is the reason for the struggle, and the difficulties, we experience? We endure lifetime after lifetime of hardships, but we also have Joy and Love. We are here to experience Emotional Freedom, and to give our Souls the opportunity to grow, and become enhanced by all the *experiences* we encounter.

We gave Free Will, and our lives are governed by our own thoughts and actions. We cannot blame another, for we are co-creators with our Divine Self, the Spirit within.

It is our Soul Purpose to be re-united with the source of All Life ~ God, or Pure, Spiritual Consciousness.

We are re-born over and over, until we reach a level of perfection, and are absorbed back into the Light. Each Sojourn upon the Earth is just another part of our Journey. All Souls are seeking to experience Unconditional Love. A New Life is A New Beginning!

Bless You.

A NEW DAY

As each New Day dawns, the Spirit re-awakens to begin anew in the Earth. It has taken a period of rest while the body *sleeps*, and journeyed back into higher realms of consciousness, where it is able to re-assess the conditions surrounding Life On Earth. Hence the saying, *Sleep on it!* This gives our Soul time to re-think and look at things from a different perspective. Every morning, all living things begin a *New Day*. We feel rested and refreshed after a good night's sleep. When this is not the case, we struggle to be at our *best*.

A few moments meditation before going to sleep will ease the transition, from a chattering mind to a peaceful one, so aiding the body to relax and drift into another dimension.

Why not pose a question to your Higher Self?

LISTEN

Listen, Children, to the small voice within. Ignore it at your peril. For stormy seas will follow, for those who continue to be deaf, dumb and blind to Spirit. You each have the key to succeed, and are equipped for your journeys. *You* have made the choices. Do not blame others for your misfortunes, but accept that *you*, and you alone, are responsible for what surrounds you. You have brought about *everything* that you have in your lives, and only *you* can change it. Others are there to facilitate, *you chose the lessons that you needed to understand and experience.* These problems that you face are merely opportunities to progress, for your Soul to grow.

Let Love flow in and out with the breath. It is the only tool you will ever need. Learn to Love yourselves, and it will lead to Love for others. If you send out Love, then it will return to you. It is the natural law ~ it must always be so. Treat yourself, and others, kindly. Speak and act with Love. And you will find that Life will run smoothly. Prayers will be answered. Go with the flow and rhythm of Life.

SPIRIT DIVINE

The Ultimate Goal is communion with The Spirit Divine: to return to The Source in perfect harmony with all ~ At-one-ment.

Each Soul has the Divine Spark within and endeavours, through many journeys, to be *At One.* This is attained through *awareness* and *self-realisation*, acknowledging the Spirit within, and from that point in time, working towards complete harmony between Heart, Mind and Spirit.

Creating balance by communicating with the Higher Self, and rising up ~ letting go of the Ego, and controlling the Emotions .

PYRAMID POWER

We are the Powers that be.
We communicate with you on all levels, in all ways known,
and unknown, to you.
As you become aware, you will be able to better understand
The Truths, to remember Who and What you are.
God is in all things.
You are God.
God is you.
He is Everything.
The Sacred Power of the Pyramid is what we would have
you link with.
Sit Quiet, Be Still, Feel it's energy.
 Ancient memories will resurface, enabling you to move on.
                  We will rejoice in the New You.

WHAT IS IT LIKE THERE AT CHRISTMAS

Much Gaiety among Friends; We Celebrate as you do.
There is no need for food and drink, unless you desire to.
We enjoy one another's company. There are Concerts of
Music, such as you have never heard before. Every fibre of
your being tingles with the sound of each note made. Such
an experience! We sing and dance and gather together.
Great Throngs of People come together in places of
Worship and Love. We Celebrate Life! The Energies are
raised on the Earth Plane, so it enables us to draw closer
still. So much Love we send to you, there are so many
places that are closed to the Light.

We emulate the Christ ~ Spirit that which is of God!

What does the future hold for Mankind?

A burning question indeed!

It is in the making.

Each Thought, every Word, every Action, every Deed, affects the future of your World.

You are creating the future *Now*!

You have been forming the future ~ since the beginning of your days.

You, The Children of God, are the Co-Creators.

It is within your power to create or destroy!

THE BREATH

The waves of the sea, as they wash over the shingle and sand, cleansing as they go, are like the Breath coursing through the Mind and Body awakening the Soul. Deep breathing accessing the dark corners of the Mind, which may have become dulled by time on the Earth. With the breath comes Light to re-activate the brain and in turn the physical body. It is like food for the lighter bodies, of which we are, for the better part of our lives, unaware. So lost, it is difficult for Man to re-establish a connection with his Higher Mind - His Higher Self.

Quiet time and contemplation is once again the key. Taking time to breathe and meditate will always bring about inner peace and calm.